THINGS YOU SHOULD KI

Things You Should Know Before I Go

Copyright 2023© by Pamela Brown-Ledet

ISBN: 978-1-7350965-5-1

Samone Publishing
infodrsamonebrown@gmail.com

samonepublishing.com

Things You Should Know Before I Go

To my dear son: a book of lessons
from a mother to her young son

PAMELA BROWN-LEDET

To Matthew: When I see you, I see the best in me.

To my mother, my angel, Mary Nelson:
You are truly the wind beneath my wings.

To my father, Jimmie Nelson:
Thank you for your love throughout the years.
Your presence has been and continues to be, everything.

To Dr. Shelia Brown:
Thank you for inspiring me to pen my thoughts. In our paths crossing,
I gained a sister for life.

To Dr. Lynda Jones Mubarak:
I am so grateful for your mentorship.
You are truly a blessing.

Dear Matthew,

After my health scare in 2011, I began to ask myself if I shared everything I needed to share with you about life up to this moment. I wrote this book to tell you what I wished I had told your 11-year-old self. This is a list of things I hope you will always remember.

Before I go, remember to...

Love your Creator with all of your heart, mind, and spirit.
Love yourself because God made you in His image.

Be your best at all times. People will remember you by how you made others feel when they met you.

Before I go, remember to...

Keep your word. Do what you say you will do. If you cannot keep a promise for any reason, make it up to that person.

Learn as much as you can in all areas of life.

Know that you make me want to be my very best.

Before I go, remember to...

Always give 100% in everything you do. Half-doing something is not an option.

When you love someone, give them your time and treasures.

When things don't go the ways you want them to go ...

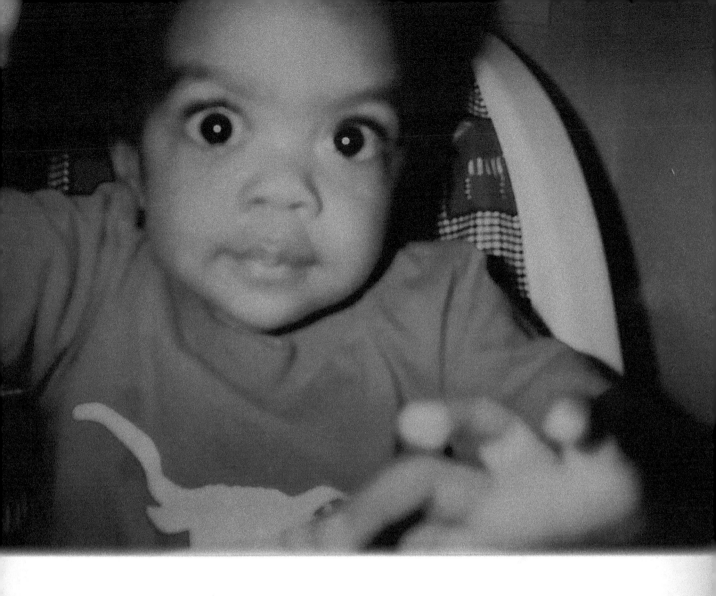

... find a reason to smile!

Before I go, remember to...

Pray and meditate daily.

When you are sick, hugs from your friends make things better.

Light up the room with your smile.

Before I go, remember to...

Always use your manners. It shows others that you value them. Open the door for strangers. Help to put dishes away too!

Before I go,

Find your purpose in life. Let it guide all you do. I found my purpose when I had you!

Love, Mom

Author Bio:

Pamela Brown-Ledet has been an educator for over two decades. Her passion is teaching young children how to enjoy reading. She has always wanted to contribute to the variety of books available to young readers. She is a two-time elementary school Teacher of the Year and District Elementary Teacher of the Year Finalist in her suburban Austin school district. Her lifelong inspiration is her son, Matthew.

CPSIA information can be obtained
at www.ICGtesting.com
Printed in the USA
BVHW010914060423
661868BV00015B/786